ABC

An Adventure Through Revelation

Shama Stock

ABC An Adventure Through Revelation
ISBN 979-8-9926951-3-7 (paperback)

© 2025 Shama Stock
Published by Fruitful Ink Press

Scripture taken from the New King James Version®. Copyright © 1982 by Thomas Nelson. Used by permission. All rights reserved.

Cover and illustrations created using AI (Midjourney version 6.1) with customized prompts.

For Kevin, Anton and Lyndon
who keep me honest and humble.
I love you forever.

"Then I saw another angel flying in the midst of heaven, having the everlasting gospel to preach to those who dwell on the earth—to every nation, tribe, tongue, and people—saying with a loud voice, 'Fear God and give glory to Him, for the hour of His judgment has come; and worship Him who made heaven and earth, the sea and springs of water.'"

Revelation 14:6-7

A is for angel

Angels are the messengers that bring the good news that Jesus loves you and wants to rescue you from sin.

"And I heard another voice from heaven saying, 'Come out of her, my people, lest you share in her sins, and lest you receive of her plagues. For her sins have reached to heaven, and God has remembered her iniquities.'"
Revelation 18:4-5

B is for Babylon

Babylon respresents a place of pride and confusion. The New Jerusalem is the city we want to live in. The humble and wise shall enter it's gates. God gives us His Word to teach us truth so we can get out of Babylon! It will soon be destroyed.

"Do not fear any of those things which you are about to suffer. ....Be faithful until death, and I will give you the crown of life."
Revelation 2:10

C is for crown

Crowns are worn by kings and by winners.
A crown is waiting for you for being faithful to Jesus.

"So the great dragon was cast out, that serpent of old,
called the Devil and Satan, who deceives the whole world;
he was cast to the earth, and his angels were cast out with him."
Revelation 12:9

D is for dragon

The dragon, or serpent, is full of deceit. He's sly and he lies and he's called the devil and Satan. Beware of friendly dragons, they are not what they seem. Jesus can protect you from his evil schemes.

"I will give of the fountain of the water of life freely to him who thirsts."
Revelation 21:6b

"For God so loved the world that He gave His only begotten Son,
that whoever believes in Him should not perish but have everlasting life."
John 3:16

E is for eternal life

Eternal life is a gift from our Father above,
given to all who will trust Him in love.

"And I saw three unclean spirits like frogs coming out of the mouth of the dragon, out of the mouth of the beast, and out of the mouth of the false prophet. For they are spirits of demons, performing signs, which go out to the kings of the earth and of the whole world, to gather them to the battle of that great day of God Almighty."

Revelation 16:13-14

F is for frogs

These three frogs symbolize spirits of devils that come out of the mouth of the dragon and his minions. They represent lies and false teachings that deceive people to fight against God Almighty. Jesus is the truth and the way. Follow Him today!

"The twelve gates were twelve pearls: each individual gate was of one pearl. And the street of the city was pure gold, like transparent glass. But I saw no temple in it, for the Lord God Almighty and the Lamb are its temple. The city had no need of the sun or of the moon to shine in it, for the glory of God illuminated it. The Lamb is its light. And the nations of those who are saved shall walk in its light, and the kings of the earth bring their glory and honor into it. Its gates shall not be shut at all by day (there shall be no night there)."
Revelation 21:21-25

G is for gate

There are twelve gates into the New Jerusalem that comes down out of heaven. Each one is a beautiful pearl. These gates stay open all day. There is no night there because Jesus is its light.

"The four living creatures, each having six wings, were full of eyes around and within. And they do not rest day or night, saying:
'Holy, holy, holy, Lord God Almighty, Who was and is and is to come!'"
Revelation 4:8

H is for holy

Holy, holy, holy, is what the angels say before God's throne. God wants us to be holy too. Jesus is the One who can make us holy through His Spirit, set apart for a special purpose.

"Jesus said to them, 'Most assuredly, I say to you, before Abraham was, I AM.'"
John 8:58

"'I am the Alpha and the Omega, the Beginning and the End,' says the Lord,
'who is and who was and who is to come, the Almighty.'"
Revelation 1:8

I is for the great I AM

Jesus is the great I AM, the beginning and the end. He was, and is, and is to come, and His love will never end!

"And I heard another from the altar saying, 'Even so, Lord God Almighty, true and righteous are Your judgments.'"
Revelation 16:7

J is for Judgment

Judgment is simply a decision made after looking at all the facts. God's judgments are true and holy and fair, so we have nothing to fear. He will give us good decision making skills [judgment] too if we humbly seek His will.

"For they are spirits of demons, performing signs, which go out to the kings of the earth and of the whole world, to gather them to the battle of that great day of God Almighty."
Revelation 16:14

"And they gathered them together to the place called in Hebrew, Armageddon. Then the seventh angel poured out his bowl into the air, and a loud voice came out of the temple of heaven, from the throne, saying, 'It is done!'"
Revelation 16:16-17

K is for the kings of the earth

The kings of the earth gather their armies to make war against God's people. But the King of kings and Lord of lords, Christ Jesus (Yeshua Messiah), wins the final battle. He is our Savior and King.

"But one of the elders said to me, 'Do not weep. Behold, the Lion of the tribe of Judah, the Root of David, has prevailed to open the scroll and to loose its seven seals.'"
Revelation 5:5

"Worthy is the Lamb who was slain
To receive power and riches and wisdom,
And strength and honor and glory and blessing!"
Revelation 5:12

L is for lamb and lion

Jesus is the perfect lamb that died to save you and wash away your sins. Jesus is also the Lion of Judah, the great King of all kings who is coming to reign. His kingdom will never end.

"For you have not come to the mountain that may be touched and that burned with fire, and blackness and tempest, and the sound of a trumpet and the voice of words, so that those who heard it begged that the word should not be spoken to them anymore. But you have come to Mount Zion and to the city of the living God, the heavenly Jerusalem...to Jesus the Mediator of the new covenant. See that you do not refuse Him who speaks."
Hebrews 12:18-19, 22-25 *paraphrased*

"And he carried me away in the Spirit to a great and high mountain, and showed me the great city, the holy Jerusalem, descending out of heaven from God,"
Revelation 21:10

M is for mountain

A great mountain burning with fire, is where God spoke words of life and words of loud warning. They didn't listen and went their own way. Sadly, it is still that way today. Now Jesus lives in Mount Zion above. He is still speaking to you with great love.

"But I have a few things against you, because you have there those who hold the doctrine of Balaam, who taught Balak to put a stumbling block before the children of Israel, to eat things sacrificed to idols, and to commit sexual immorality. Thus you also have those who hold the doctrine of the Nicolaitans, which thing I hate."
Revelation 2:14-15

N is for Nicolaitan

Followers of Nicolas, a leader gone astray. They do deeds that God hates like the sneaky prophet Balaam of old. He convinced foreign women to invite God's people to pagan feasts and immoral parties. God called this unfaithfulness.

"Then Samuel took the horn of oil and anointed him in the midst of his brothers; and the Spirit of the Lord came upon David from that day forward."
1 Samuel 16:13a

"And do not harm the oil and the wine."
Revelation 6:6

O is for oil

Oil is for anointing a priest or a king to serve God in holiness and do the right thing. God sends His Spirit to anoint you too, and help you know the best things to do.

"And God will wipe away every tear from their eyes; there shall be no more death, nor sorrow, nor crying. There shall be no more pain, for the former things have passed away."
Revelation 21:4

P is for Paradise

Paradise is the place where God lives. He wants to take you there to eat from the tree of life. He will wipe away all tears. There will be no more crying or pain there.

"And he cried mightily with a loud voice, saying,
'Babylon the great is fallen, is fallen...'
And I heard another voice from heaven saying, 'Come out of her, my people, lest
you share in her sins, and lest you receive of her plagues. For her sins have
reached to heaven, and God has remembered her iniquities.'"
Revelation 18:2a, 4-5

"In the measure that she glorified herself and lived luxuriously, in the same
measure give her torment and sorrow; for she says in her heart, 'I sit as queen,
and am no widow, and will not see sorrow.'"
Revelation 18:7

Q is for queen

A title given to Babylon and a symbol of all worship that is proud and against the ways of the God of heaven. She thinks she is indestructible, but she will fall and be destroyed.

"As many as I love, I rebuke and chasten.
Therefore be zealous and repent."
Revelation 3:19

"There is joy in the presence of the angels of God
over one sinner who repents."
Luke 15:10

R is for repentance

Repentance is admitting when you've done wrong and asking Jesus to help you be strong. It's turning away from sin and letting your new life begin.

"After these things I heard a loud voice of a great multitude in heaven, saying, 'Alleluia! Salvation and glory and honor and power belong to the Lord our God!'"
Revelation 19:1

S is for salvation

Jesus died in your place on the cross. He came to save you from the destruction of sin and give you eternal life. He loves you so much.

"These are the ones who come out of the great tribulation, and washed their robes and made them white in the blood of the Lamb."
Revelation 7:14

"These things I have spoken to you, that in Me you may have peace. In the world you will have tribulation; but be of good cheer, I have overcome the world."
John 16:33

T is for tribulation

We may face trouble and persecution when we choose to follow God. This sinful world is full of sadness, but Jesus can bring you peace and gladness.

"He who has an ear, let him hear what the Spirit says to the churches."
Revelation 3:22

U is for understanding

Understanding is what comes from above. It is sent through the Spirit from our heavenly Father with love.

"And I saw something like a sea of glass mingled with fire, and those who have the victory over the beast, over his image and over his mark and over the number of his name, standing on the sea of glass, having harps of God."
Revelation 15:2

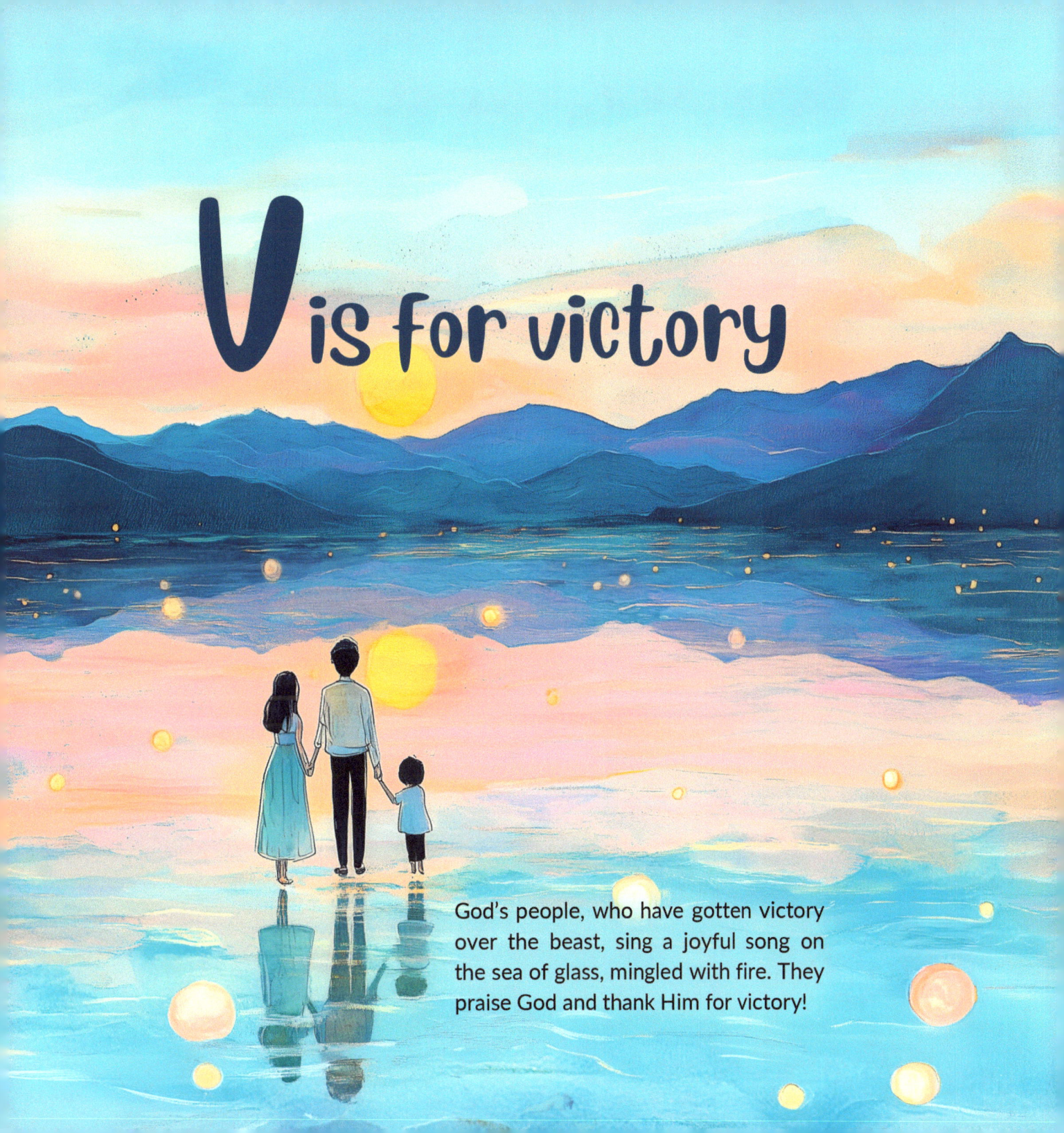

V is for victory

God's people, who have gotten victory over the beast, sing a joyful song on the sea of glass, mingled with fire. They praise God and thank Him for victory!

"He who overcomes shall be clothed in white garments, and I will not blot out his name from the Book of Life; but I will confess his name before My Father and before His angels."
Revelation 3:5

W is for white

White is a symbolic color of purity and holiness. Jesus promises to wash our sins away and give us His white robe of righteousness.

"Here is wisdom. Let him who has understanding calculate the number of the beast, for it is the number of a man: His number is 666."
Revelation 13:18

X is for the last letter in six

666 is the number of man who has chosen his own way. Six is just short of seven which will make us complete, when we rest in God's love, in His ways, on His days. We rest from our six days of work as God did from His, and receive salvation through His mercy and grace.

"Blessed and holy is he who has part in the first resurrection. Over such the second death has no power, but they shall be priests of God and of Christ, and shall reign with Him a thousand years."
Revelation 20:6

Y is for 1,000 Years

The first resurrection brings safety and rest for those whose names are written in the book of life. The second death has no power over them. They will live and reign with Christ for a thousand years.

"And I heard the number of those who were sealed. One hundred and forty-four thousand of all the tribes of the children of Israel were sealed:
...of the tribe of Zebulun twelve thousand were sealed;"
Revelation 7:4, 8a

"Now He who establishes us with you in Christ and has anointed us is God, who also has sealed us and given us the Spirit in our hearts as a guarantee."
2 Corinthian 1:21-22

Z is for Zebulun

Zebulun is one of the twelve tribes of Israel, sealed with the seal of the living God. We are adopted into God's family when we believe in Jesus and are sealed with the Holy Spirit of promise. We are all one in Christ Jesus. Hallelujah, Amen!

For children's bible studies on the book of Revelation visit
revelationforkids.com

www.ingramcontent.com/pod-product-compliance
Lightning Source LLC
Chambersburg PA
CBHW041553120626
46551CB00002B/193